Dedicated to William Rasey

Time Bandits

11
Fls.
Obs.
B♭ Cls.
B. Cls.
Bsns.
A. Sxs.
mf
T. Sxs.
B. Sx.
11
B♭ Tpts. 1 2
Hns.
mf
Tbns.
mf
Euphs.
mf
Tubas
mf
Timp.
Bells
Mba. (or Bells)
Xyl.
S. D.
S. D. H. H. B. D.
Perc. 1 2
9
10
11
12
13
14
15

Fls.
Obs.
B♭ Cls.
B. Cls.
Bsns.
A. Sxs.
T. Sxs.
B. Sx.
B♭ Tpts.
Hns.
Tbns.
Euphs.
Tubas
Timp.
Bells
Mba. (or Bells)
Xyl.
S. D. H. H. B. D.
Perc.
17
a2
Tam-tam
16
17
18
19
20
21
22

25
Fls.
Obs.
B♭ Cls.
div.
B. Cls.
Bsns.
A. Sxs.
mf
T. Sxs.
B. Sx.
25
B♭ Tpts. 1 2
Hns.
Tbns.
Euphs.
Tubas
Timp.
Bells
Mba. (or Bells)
Xyl.
S. D. H. H. B. D.
Perc. 1 2
23
24
25
26
27
28

FULL SCORE

Time Bandits

Brian L. Monroe

INSTRUMENTATION

1-FULL SCORE
6-FLUTE
2-OBOE
12-CLARINET in Bb
2-BASS CLARINET in Bb
2-BASSOON
4-ALTO SAXOPHONE in Eb
2-TENOR SAXOPHONE in Bb
1-BARITONE SAXOPHONE in Eb
5-1st TRUMPET in Bb
5-2nd TRUMPET in Bb
4-HORN in F
6-TROMBONE
2-EUPHONIUM in Treble Clef
3-EUPHONIUM in Bass Clef
4-TUBA
1-TIMPANI
1-ORCHESTRA BELLS
1-MARIMBA (or Orchestra Bells)
1-XYLOPHONE
3-SNARE DRUM, HIHAT, and BASS DRUM
3-PERCUSSION 1: Ratchet, Triangle, Tam-tam, and Suspended Cymbal
1-PERCUSSION 2: Temple Blocks

Grade 1
Duration: Approx. 2 Minutes

Southern MUSIC

The “Time Bandits” travel through musical performing time, wreaking havoc and instability in their wake. Measures turn up missing one or even two beats as the bandits try to trip up the student performers. Occasionally, the bandits drop a stolen beat and it finds its way into a measure that suddenly has five beats instead of the normal four. The bandits have been known to unleash their most fearsome weapon, the dreaded *senza tempus*, which annihilates music and beat, creating total silence. How long can it last?

About the Composer

Brian L. Monroe has been a music educator with over thirty years of experience with concert band, jazz ensemble, marching band, and music theory/history from fifth grade through high school. His bands were honored at state and national levels and he is active as a clinician and adjudicator. He holds degrees from Kent State University where he studied percussion with Michael Burritt and composition with Thomas Janson and Walter Watson. He also studied with J. Rex Mitchell.

Performance Suggestions

The temple blocks represent time, in the sense of a clock providing a steady beat pattern. Note that the pattern remains constant so that less experienced audience members can hear the disruptions in time. The opening ratchet signifies winding up the spring in a non-electric clock. Despite the humorous nature of the work, always remind students that melody, balance, and blend must remain foremost in their attention.

31
Fls.
Obs.
B♭ Cls.
B. Cls.
Bsns.
A. Sxs.
T. Sxs.
B. Sx.
B♭ Tpts. 1 2
Hns.
Tbns.
Euphs.
Tubas
Timp.
Bells
Mba. (or Bells)
Xyl.
S. D.
H. H.
B. D.
Perc. 1 2
Sus. Cym.
Tam-tam
Sus. Cym.
Tam-tam
29
30
31
32
33
34
35

G. P.
37
39
43
Fls.
Obs.
B♭ Cls.
B. Cls.
Bsns.
A. Sxs.
T. Sxs.
B. Sx.
B♭ Tpts. 1 2
a2
Hns.
Tbns.
Euphs.
Tubas
Timp.
Bells
Mba. (or Bells)
Xyl.
S. D.
H. H.
B. D.
Tri.
Perc. 1 2
36
37
38
39
40
41
42
43

Fls.
Obs.
B♭ Cls.
B. Cls.
Bsns.
A. Sxs.
T. Sxs.
f
B. Sx.
B♭ Tpts. 1 2
a2
a2
Hns.
Tbns.
f
Euphs.
f
Tubas
Timp.
Bells
Mba. (or Bells)
Xyl.
S. D.
H. H.
B. D.
Perc. 1 2
p
p
f
p
44
45
46
47
48
49

53
Fls.
Obs.
B♭ Cls.
div.
B. Cls.
Bsns.
A. Sxs.
T. Sxs.
B. Sx.
53
B♭ Tpts. 1 2
a2
Hns.
Tbns.
Euphs.
Tubas
Timp.
Bells
Mba. (or Bells)
Xyl.
S. D. H. H. B. D.
Perc. 1 2
50
51
52
53
54
55

Fls.
Obs.
B♭ Cls.
B. Cls.
Bsns.
A. Sxs.
T. Sxs.
B. Sx.
B♭ Tpts. 1 2
Hns.
Tbns.
Euphs.
Tubas
Timp.
Bells
Mba. (or Bells)
Xyl.
S. D. H. H. B. D.
Perc. 1 2
div.
a2
56
57
58
59
60
61
62

Southern® MUSIC
Exclusively Distributed By
HAL•LEONARD®

U.S. $7.00
1 96288 20952 2
S1057FS
HL01455421

EAN 13
9 798892 702966